Late $_{\text{the}}^{\text{to}}$ Harvest

Late _{to the} Harvest

One Man's Journey from
Suffering To Salvation

DON DUBOIS

ISBN: 979-8-90252-077-1   (Paperback)
ISBN: 979-8-90252-076-4   (Hardcover)
ISBN: 979-8-90252-075-7   (eBook)

Printed in the United States of America

CONTENTS

To Nancy

Thank you for bringing me back to God

SYNOPSIS

This book chronicles my journey back to Christ during a season of severe illness. The story draws from my life experiences, past and present. It highlights my needs and my willingness to turn to God and to the roots of my Catholic faith in pursuit of wellness and wholeness. This book relies heavily on supporting material written by Matthew Kelly and Oswald Chambers. I hope that I have written a book of hope, direction, and enlightenment for those facing illnesses of their own.

ONE

Mentors and Advisors

Anyone can name, off the top of their head, the five most important people in their lives. We can all point to literary giants who have influenced us through their writings. Authors such as Jules Verne, Washington Irving, Charles Dickens, Mark Twain, and Herman Melville were among my favorites, who shaped and molded my early development. Later in life, writers such as Winston Churchill, J. D. Salinger, Jeff Shaara, Robert Frost, and Pope John Paul II left their marks on me as well.

Literary giants certainly influenced my imagination, but it is our immediate surroundings—and the people who inhabit them—that influence us most deeply. One such example was Fr. Gene Barrette, a man who entered my life at just the right time to rescue a lost boy from certain perdition.

Fr. Gene may have been an anomaly in the Catholic Church. I could recount his many accomplishments within that institution, including his time working in the Vatican under Pope John Paul II. But the true importance of this man, and the enduring role he chose to play in my life, is defined not by his titles or associations but by his decision to remain my lifelong friend and confidant.

His parents, elderly even then, lived next door to my mother and me in Connecticut. My father had left my mother and brother for another woman. Back then, everyone in the neighborhood knew I was being raised fatherless, one of many children growing up in a broken household. The elderly Barrettes made it their mission to keep an eye on me while my mother was away at work. That's how it was back then: people in the old neighborhood looked out for one another. People really did mind each other's business.

Their son Gene—whom everyone called Gino—had recently been ordained a priest in the Catholic Church. One summer, he returned home to oversee the painting of his parents' house. I was perhaps ten or twelve years old at the time. Finding me at home alone and without any occupation, he invited me to help with the task.

Gino, a young man in his mid- to late twenties, was a sight to behold. He did not fit the mold of a Catholic priest in the 1960s and early 1970s. His long, straight brown hair was parted in the middle and fell past his shoulders. He wore full facial hair—a beard and moustache—well kept and neatly trimmed. His smile was commanding, contagious, and always at the ready. He was articulate and intelligent and spoke in quiet tones. In these respects, he was the opposite of my parents in every way.

Gino was witty and inviting. He could play the piano and sing in several languages. He was everything I aspired to be and more. But during that particular summer week, all he wanted me to be was his painting assistant, and all he could afford to offer in return was breakfast and lunch if I chose to join him. Looking back, I would have paid for the privilege of spending time with a man I held in such high esteem. Even at twelve, I understood that I would gain something far more valuable than money—or even experience—by giving myself to the task.

Bright and early the following day, a relationship began that would last a lifetime, despite half a world of separation. Their house was a modest two-bedroom home in a lower- to middle-income neighborhood. The color chosen was close to its previous hue, a blend of gold and mustard yellow. It would not have been my choice, but then again, the house we lived in had not seen paint for as long as I had been alive.

Typically, most of my friends in the neighborhood—other adolescent boys like me—would not have given Fr. Gene the time of day, much less lent him a hand in such an endeavor. But I was glad to be part of it for many reasons, especially because Fr. Gene loved to sing, and I loved listening to him.

I will never forget sitting beside him on wooden staging, side by side, slapping paint on clapboards under the hot summer sun. Quite often, Fr. Gene would erupt in song, belting out show tunes and other selections with which I was wholly unacquainted. It was a musical smorgasbord, though on occasion he would stumble upon a tune with which I was familiar. I can still hear his clear voice ringing through the neighborhood: "Who can take a sunrise, sprinkle it with dew, cover it with chocolate and a miracle or two? The Candy Man, oh, the Candy Man can, the Candy Man can 'cause he mixes it with love and makes the world taste good."

Always striving to look on the bright side of life, this song meant a great deal to me. I loved its imagery.

I knew I liked sunrises and dew, and who didn't like chocolate? I already believed in miracles because I had experienced so many in my short life. And I knew that mixing anything with love made it better. To a twelve-year-old boy, it seemed the very language of God. Right then and there, I felt certain I had found my calling: I would grow up to become a Catholic priest.

We spent three glorious days together painting that house. They were days full of sunshine, mirth, good song, pasta and meatballs, and cherry pie topped with whipped cream. It was all so wonderful and so good. From that moment on, our relationship began to grow and blossom and would span more than half a century. It's a story I love to share with anyone willing to listen.

Gino went on to live the life of Fr. Gene Barrette, and later that summer, he celebrated his first Mass at St. James Parish, where I attended. We weren't exactly a churchgoing family. As far back as memory serves, my parents intended to raise my brother and me in the Catholic tradition. I think they began with good intentions, but something went amiss, and they stopped attending. If I recollect correctly, my mother may have noticed another woman making eyes at my father one Sunday morning, and that was all the excuse she needed. From then on, they never saw the inside of that church again.

But for me, it was too late. I was already hooked. I loved the Catholic Mass. I had already memorized the entire ceremony: the priest's liturgy, the Apostle's Creed, the Lord's Prayer, the Hail Mary, as well as the responsorials. I enjoyed being in church, and I missed it terribly after my parents stopped going. So, on my own, I would rise every Sunday morning, wash my face, comb my hair, put on my best clothes, and ride my bicycle to St. James Church, where I sat at the very end of the first pew directly before the altar.

I will forever remember that fateful Sunday morning when, lifting my eyes to the altar, there stood Fr. Gene. I was awestruck! I imagine my mouth must have fallen open when I first spied him in his shimmering vestments, and I must have flushed red when he acknowledged me with a smile. In that moment, I could have died and gone to heaven!

The congregation present that Sunday morning will also recall that they witnessed a very nontraditional Mass, perhaps the first of its kind in the parish. To me, Fr. Gene appeared the very embodiment of Jesus Christ Himself, with his long flowing hair parted in the middle, his closely trimmed beard, and his white flowing robes. But beyond that, Fr. Gene proceeded to cast aside the rest of the traditional Mass.

He stepped from behind the altar and proceeded down the aisle of the Church, from where he delivered his homily. This was simply unheard of back then. No churchgoer had ever seen anything like it, at least not here in stuffy old New England! But there he was, mingling with the congregation, proclaiming a message of change, brotherhood, and tolerance. I recall the silence as he spoke. It seemed no one dared to breathe. But I did! This man was more than God's messenger. This man was my friend, and I wanted everyone to know it!

That summer eventually passed, and Fr. Gene began his long career in the Catholic Church. I returned to my life as I knew it, though forever changed by the influence of a very special man. Never diminish the power of one bright light shining in the dark. That light changed my life and gave me new direction, as I'm sure it did for countless others. Fr. Gene went on to touch the lives of millions around the world. But in all of that, he never failed to remain faithful to our friendship, as he continued to endear himself to me in so many ways over the years.

Given the weighty responsibilities he carried during his career as superior general of the Missionaries of Our Lady of La Salette from 1982 to 1988, it was always a wonder to me that he found time to keep in touch. It was always a treat to hear from Fr. Gene. I never knew from where in the world he might write, and my wanderlust found vicarious nourishment through his travels. But I could always count on at least one letter from him around the holidays.

One particular letter remains close and dear to my heart. It arrived just before winter break while I was in college, postmarked Citta' Del Vaticano Posta Aerea. My roommate had picked up the mail—a light envelope postmarked "The Vatican." As he handed me my mail, he asked, "Who's sending you a letter from the Vatican?"

I answered, "Why, the Pope of course! Would you like to hear what he has to say?"

"The Pope?" he asked again.

"Yes, the Pope." I nodded.

It wasn't entirely a lie, for I half expected at any moment to receive tremendous news from Rome:

> My dearest Donald,
>
> Greetings from the Vatican! You will be delighted to learn that once again, the white smoke has cast its long shadow across St. Peter's Basilica, and unbeknownst to me, I have become the newly elected Pope, the Keeper of the Flame, the latest disciple of Christ. I wanted you to be the first to know. Hope all is well with you.
>
> Love,
> Fr. Gene

But alas, this is what he actually wrote:

Dear Don,

A few days ago, I returned from two months in Latin America—Brazil and Argentina—to visit our communities there and do some work with them. Your letter was waiting for me and what a joy it was to read it. I only regret that we are so many miles apart, but so many of the things you had to say would merit many hours of sharing and exploring together.

First of all let me say how happy I am to hear how things are going for you—and also to read about your own self-awareness concerning your own growth. That is so very important and special. It's also good to always bear in mind that our lives do have that kind of pattern—at times we seem to grow at leaps and bounds, and at other times we just seem to plod along. But often, it's the plodding that produces the most enduring growth.

Don, your questions about a vocation are very thought provoking. Vocations demand discernment—demand a certain kind of time and space within ourself so that we can <u>hear</u> who is calling and what we are being called to do. A vocation is not something we can force, nor something we can manipulate, at least not if it is to be authentic. It is like a seed planted within us—its growth and fruit depends a great deal upon the way we nurture and care for it— but its existence is quite independent of us—it is from the Lord.

At your age it is true that we want to walk into the world and contribute what we can to efforts for peace and justice. Thank God there are those desires in youth. But remember Don, our work for world peace and love and brotherhood will always begin, and often end, in the small circle that we call our world—the places and people that we know and can concretely serve.

Mother Teresa of Calcutta, India and her community of Sisters and Brothers has not been able to wipe out the poverty and misery in India and other parts of the world—but they have been able to bring Christ's healing and gentle touch and love to the people they meet. So too, you must slowly recognize the small area in the world that you can touch—and even if it is unseen by you, never forget that the touch of your love and care sends ripples throughout the universe, as a touch on a pond sends ripples across it.

And most beautiful of all, remember that the good we can do, the love we can bring, is the power and presence of the Lord and Spirit in us. And that alone should give us courage, especially when we see and recognize our own limitations, weaknesses, and failings. So don't stop listening—try to discern where the Lord wants for you, how to best incarnate His love in the unique person that is you, because basically, that is the fundamental vocation—to make Jesus live in and through us. He's in us, we just have to find the way to "enflesh" him.

> Don, please keep in touch. You are in my prayers
> and thoughts. Much love in the Lord, Fr. Gene.
> PS. "May you stand firm against anything that
> may try to discourage you from attaining full
> maturity in Christ." John Paul II

And without another word between us, my roommate turned and walked away. I folded the letter from Fr. Gene, placed it back in its envelope, and slipped it into my pocket for safekeeping.

Fr. Gene is the kind of friend, the kind of human influence, for which we all pray. I do not know why God chose to bless me with such a friendship so early in life, but I believe He knew I needed it more than anyone else. Indeed, He knew, because it was in my early adolescent years that I could have gone either way, and partly because of Gino's love for me, I chose right. Very few people came out of the old neighborhood so blessed.

Fr. Gene wasn't the only major influence in my life. In fact, there were many others, far too numerous to mention here. But one who deserves special recognition is my old high school guidance counselor, with whom I remained in contact throughout life. Her name was Mary Morris, formerly Sister Mary Morris. She had retired from her vocation as a nun to become a public school teacher, for reasons I never knew. Mary Morris was a strange figure within the public school system, as anyone who knew her would attest. She wasn't just my guidance counselor; she also taught an advanced placement social studies course that I took for college credit.

I must admit, I never gained much from her lectures, but I did learn a great deal about life in general from her. Her experiences were broad and diverse, and she had a penchant for sharing them with her students. So there we sat, perhaps a dozen in all, listening to her didactic lectures filled with long-lost childhood experiences, loosely tied to the rise of and fall of Western civilizations. She drove most of the students to tears—tears of boredom, that is—with her wide-ranging asides and personal treatises. But for me, her lectures were entirely different. I may not have cared as much as the others about the rise and fall of Western civilizations, but I did care about Mary Morris and her life's experiences, and I found them quite fascinating.

Ms. Morris seemed to really enjoy telling stories about her mischievous youth, and her knack of organizing student boycotts, sit-ins, and other rebellious activities. She cast herself as a real rabble-rouser intent on upsetting the status quo. That is what I admired most about her, and it was what drew me to her. But it wasn't her qualities or quirky personality that changed my life. No, it was instead one single sentence she spoke to me in one private session. I heard those words only once, but they rocked me to the core. And I happened to be listening.

One day, we were in her office discussing my plans for the future—specifically, which colleges I might apply to in the fall and what my concentration might be. I must have looked somewhat perplexed because eventually she leaned toward me and asked, "What's the matter?"

After a brief hesitation, I replied, "I don't think I'm going to college."

"Why not?" she asked.

"Well," I explained, "I live alone with my mother, and she can't afford to send me. We don't have any money."

I'll never forget how the look on that lady's face changed. She rocked forward in her seat, rested her arms on the desk, and looked me squarely in the eye. Then came the most significant words I had ever heard:

"Donald," she said earnestly, "don't worry about the money. Get accepted first, and the money will follow."

Let the meaning of that statement sink in. Here I was, a teenager without a father figure, raised by a single mother with two boys, working in a food processing plant for less than a hundred dollars a week. Where, exactly, would the money come from? And yet I believed her. After all, she was my high school counselor.

That one sentence, more than any other words spoken in my presence, changed my life in profound and lasting ways. I did get accepted to college, and the money did follow—more than I needed.

But even more important, I have applied that exact philosophy to every investment I have made since, sometimes with reckless abandonment! That is how much I believed in her wisdom. She spoke the truth.

I'm not sure she even understood the full meaning of her own words. They apply not only to under-privileged high school students seeking higher education but also to entrepreneurial minds searching for capital to launch new and daring ventures. With her guidance, I came to understand that everything in this world is created twice: first in the imagination, then in reality. But how many good ideas die as seeds in the womb, never to see the light of day, never to become flesh on the bones, because of lack of capital?

That's all balderdash. Why? Because there's so much money in the world it can never be counted! Lack of money is never the real problem. Money flows naturally to good ideas. It's a physical law like gravity. It has to! It's been said that if the dream is big enough, the facts don't count. IF THE DREAM IS BIG ENOUGH, THE FACTS DON'T COUNT!

Once I realized the truth of that statement, I began to dream bigger and bigger dreams. Dreaming without limits can be a lot of fun. It can also be frightening for some. For example, if time and money were no object, what would you do with the rest of your life? Allow your mind to run with that idea for a moment. Don't be afraid—it's only a simple mental exercise. But for some, imagining on that level is a difficult, if not impossible.

If time and money were no object, what would you do with the rest of your life? If you're in high school, would you apply to Harvard? If you're working as a waitress, would you open the restaurant you've always dreamed about? Or would you travel the world with your family, teaching them history and geography firsthand? If you're retired, would you volunteer with a Christian relief organization? Or would you finally take a long-deserved vacation? The choices are endless, but you need to choose what you want to do, and that takes discernment and vision.

I believe Ms. Morris understood all of that, and in so far as she did, she tried to impress it upon me—and fortunately, I got it. I was fortunate, because most of my friends never did, and many still don't. Most lead lives of quiet desperation, confined by their own imagination and their unwillingness to step out. Stepping out means risking failure, and failure can be embarrassing. But in reality, embarrassment is simply caring what others think of you, and I learned through experience that what others think of me doesn't amount to a hill of beans.

Fr. Gene. Sister Mary Morris. My mother. Everything I hold to be true and good about people, and about life itself, I attribute to Fr. Gene. Everything I know about risk-taking and reaching for the stars began with Sister Mary's admonitions. And everything I know about grit and determination I learned from my mother, who raised two boys alone. In highlighting the influence these three had on my life, I risk overlooking and minimizing the impact of so many others. It goes without saying that everyone we encounter influences us in some way. Even those who may have influenced us negatively—whether through good intentions or bad—likely provided the life experiences we needed, without which we might have become obdurate.

TWO

Bound By Chains of Unbelief

One sure sign that you live in bondage is that you try to live independent of God. It amazes me how many people believe they can live without God in their lives! The idea is preposterous. All you need to do is look around, glance at the heavens at night or at the trees by day, to know there is a true God, the Creator of our universe. For me, it's that simple.

From time to time I pause to contemplate the limitless, infinite universe. Most people I know will agree the universe is infinite, but when pressed, they cannot explain what they mean. The truth is, we cannot fully grasp the limitlessness of space no matter how hard we try. When you stop to contemplate the infinite universe as something beyond space and time, things can get pretty scary.

The human mind tries to impose boundaries and dimensions on everything it sees, and it has great difficulty comprehending the ever-expanding, boundless universe. Whenever I try to comprehend a hundred billion galaxies, my mind begins to swim. It's as if my mind can "almost capture" the thought of infinite space and time, but then it suddenly implodes back into its everyday, well-defined little world. Is it just me, or is it something really incomprehensible?

Oswald Chambers writes:

> It is nonsense to imagine that God expects me
> to discern all that is clear to His own mind, all
> He asks of me is to maintain perfect confidence

in Himself. Faith springs from the indwelling
of the life of God in me.[1]

As human beings, we tend to think in dimensions and in ways that we can quantify things. We like to have everything neat, organized, and parceled out. An acre, for example, is 43,560 ft^2. A mile is 5,280 linear feet. An hour is sixty minutes, a minute is sixty seconds, and a nanosecond is one-billionth of a second—the time it takes for light to travel about a foot.

If you find that you have a hard time contemplating the ever-expanding universe, then try to think in terms of nanoseconds. What can happen in a nanosecond? That's a billion times faster than the blink of an eye. It really requires a quantum jump in our ability to even think about it. Allow your mind to wander for a minute, and you may find yourself travelling "beyond the boundaries of our universe," or conversely you may find yourself focusing on quarks, the elementary particles of matter (until scientists discover the next smaller universal constituent).

I finally realized after much mental tribulation that it was easy to understand the universe if you understood God. An infinite God can create an infinite universe. An infinite God provides us all with infinite love, infinite forgiveness, and infinite mercy. Big or small, far or near, God is everywhere. For as long as I can remember, I've been aware that God is real and that He is near. Someone once told me that the power of prayer eases the burden and speeds the results. I remember hearing those words a long time ago and thinking to myself, *That's what I want: to ease the burden and to speed the results.*

In part, I am where I am today because of my prayer life—but more on that later. God does not always answer my prayers when I want Him to, or in the ways that I expect. But one thing I know for sure: God will always answer my prayers according to His will. When I choose to believe in God, He helps me believe in myself, and by believing in both Him and myself, it becomes easier for me

---

1   Chambers, *The Complete Works of Oswald Chambers*, 970

to believe in others. By believing in yourself and others, you can participate in loving cooperation as part of a team. No man is an island; no one should have to go it alone. But if you're without God, that's exactly what happens. You find yourself going through life all alone because no one can trust in you. I've heard it said, "He who is untrusting is also untrustworthy." Trust in God.

So to be truly happy, we must first trust in God. From that core belief, all good things follow. Instead of a life weighed down by misery and worry, we can enjoy peace of mind and contentment. A life of bondage is a life of loneliness; freedom from bondage brings many good gifts. People living in bondage are not only spiritually starved but also starved for time. By contrast, people I know who live by God's standards seem to have an abundance of both time and material resources. They gladly share what they have with others and remain content with what is theirs.

Belief in God is a decision. It's a decision to move from a self-centered existence toward an existence centered on others. Every time I answer the phone, no matter where I am or what I am doing, I always say, "Hello, this is Don DuBois. May I help you?" I enjoy being of service. I've heard it said that if you help enough people get what they want in life, you will, in turn, receive what you want. It's a proven natural law, as certain as gravity.

But I do not expect anything in return when I give to others. I give of myself because it's the right thing to do and because it brings joy. When you give from the heart, God's blessings return—piled high, shaken together, and overflowing. Jesus taught us to treat others as we would like to be treated. That truth has endured for two thousand years; it is no secret, though many still fail to recognize it for what it is.

Fr. Gene saw it clearly and lived his life accordingly. He served as a great role model for me and continues to do so. He was there to lift me up when I was down. But I'm certain there were times when Fr. Gene was down too, and in those dark moments, on whom did he rely? When you find yourself alone, in the darkest recesses of your mind, to whom do you turn? At times like that, I've come to the realization that all I have—and all I've really ever had—is God.

When you reach the point in life where you understand that all you have is God, I believe you've finally arrived. Life becomes worth living, and worth living to the fullest. Once you rely on God, there are no limits on what you can do or who you can become. With God, all things become possible.

My high school guidance counselor knew this truth as well. She was a woman of faith. "Get accepted first," she said, "and the money will follow." That is a simple statement of faith full of wisdom and truth. Her simple words propelled me to greater heights. I often reflect on the profound impact she had on my life. I have been able to pass her wisdom on to others I have encountered. Like ripples across the lake, our lives touch others, stretching outward in all directions into infinity.

THREE

What Do I Believe?

September 18, 2012

Today, I read in a newsfeed that scientists are close to "proving that there is no God." What an utterly contemptible statement. I could not bear to even read the words a second time. What person could willfully compose such a sentence? I was left speechless. But then I remembered I had God, and suddenly I felt deep sorrow for the person who had written the article.

My heart reached out to that individual, longing to draw him into the loving embrace of God's love. People simply don't know because they do not seek, and therefore they never find. They do not knock, so the door is never opened to them. They do not ask, so they never receive the answers they so desperately need—the very answers God longs to give. God wants us to know. God wants us to feel. God wants us to receive the gifts He would bestow upon us. But you have to first seek, ask, and knock.

Every man or woman can choose to believe or not to believe. Choice is not about proof; it is a decision between belief and unbelief. Eventually, we must all ask ourselves, "What do I believe?" For me, the proof is everywhere that God is real. The Spirit of God dwells within me, and I feel His presence coursing through me. I believe in God when I look at my wife and children. I see His very existence when I look at a tree or the clouds in the sky. What more proof could anyone need?

I suppose you could read the arguments put forth by C. S. Lewis in his book *The Case for Christianity,* but even that requires a leap of faith—faith enough to open the book. In the end, we all find what we're looking for. I'm looking for true love, and without God among us, there can be no true love among us. There are few things in life of which I am certain, but of this I am sure: God loves me, and I love God, and that has made all the difference in my life.

For the past two decades, I have prayed almost every day the prayer of Jabez, found in the Old Testament (NIV):

> Jabez was more honorable than his brother. His mother had named him Jabez, saying, "I have given birth to him in pain." Jabez cried out to the God of Israel, "Oh, that You would bless me and enlarge my territory! Let Your hand be with me and keep me from harm so that I will be free from pain." So God granted his request. (1 Chronicles 4:9–10)

I have found strength and reassurance in this simple prayer. Perhaps that is what it takes—a simple prayer. God has indeed enlarged my territory! But there is no person less deserving of His blessings than me, and still He has come to my rescue time and again. I've often wondered why. Don't get me wrong. I am grateful, and I've thanked God from the bottom of my heart on countless occasions. Still, I realized that I still carry the "guilt" of feeling so unworthy of His love.

I bore that sense of "unworthiness" for the next thirteen years, until God finally decided He had enough of my pitiful self-loathing. In 2025, God reached me in a way that only He could. I was about to enter the darkest time of my life, and it would require a quantum leap of faith to move beyond where I was. It became a journey from suffering to salvation, drawing me closer to God than I had ever been. But first, I had to cast the devil out of my life.

FOUR

Moving Closer To God

October 17, 2025

Perhaps that's it then—a simple prayer. God has blessed me throughout my life despite my sinful ways. It's been thirteen years since I wrote that sentence—thirteen years of living, working, raising a family, and growing older. And during much of that time, I paid little attention to God. I stopped going to church and made a habit of socializing with friends in bars.

I told myself I was a social drinker, not an alcoholic. I once asked my doctor what the definition of an alcoholic was. He said, "Well, clinically speaking, if you have more than two drinks a day, you're an alcoholic." Then he asked me, "How many do you have?" I answered, "Two."

What changed over those thirteen years? My mentor and advisor passed away. Fr. Gene died of cancer five years ago. Before his death, he visited my wife and me one last time. He had lost all his hair and was only a shadow of his former self. Chemotherapy had slowly drained his vitality. We went out to dinner at a local restaurant and spoke about many things, about life in general. It was hard to see him so diminished. I was at a loss for words, realizing I was losing one of my dearest friends—someone who had had a profound and lasting effect on my life. It was the last time I saw him. He died shortly thereafter.

Before he died, he produced a historical video of his life, narrated in his own voice. It pays lasting tribute to the man and his life, and I frequently watch it. It acts as my lifeline to the man who once saved a teenage boy from a life of utter ruin. I shudder to think where I might have ended up without Fr. Gene's influence. With his passing, I lost one of the brightest guiding lights of my life. He is sorely missed. He touched thousands of souls, not just my own.

I wish he were here by my side even now. In a way, he still is. I reach out to him often in my prayers, and I know he can hear me. I believe he is smiling down on me even as I write these thoughts down on paper. He is one of many who have loved me in this life, and I believe he still does. Even now, when I close my eyes, I can see his smile and hear his gentle words. Upon his death, Fr. Gene was buried at the La Salette Shrine (Sanctuaire Notre-Dame de La Salette), high in the French Alps. Following my recent illness, I feel a renewed urgency to visit there soon.

In August 2025, I fell off a health cliff. I became terribly sick—unable to eat, unable to sleep, unable to work, and relegated to the couch. God had gotten a hold of me, and there was nothing I could do but pay attention to what He was trying to say. I was willing to go wherever He led me, even unto death. During that time, I truly believed I was going to die.

Basically, I had suffered an extreme anxiety attack. The medication I had taken for ten years stopped working; my body had simply grown accustomed to it. In Connecticut, we endured a hot, humid August with four heat waves back to back. When it gets hot and humid, I get touchy. The stifling nights robbed me of a good night's sleep, and the lack of sleep disrupted my body's chemical balance.

It turned out my serotonin levels were totally out of balance. Serotonin is a crucial neurotransmitter and hormone that affects sleep cycles, appetite, digestion, memory, social behavior, and sexual function. About 90 percent of the body's serotonin is produced in the gut, where it also influences bowel movements and the gut-brain axis. I was unaware of any of this when my health crisis began.

Taking melatonin as a sleep aid didn't help; no amount of herbal teas and other natural remedies seemed to do the trick. In addition, I had watched my brother die of colorectal cancer two years earlier, and I feared I was destined to be another victim of that terrible disease. I really believed I was dying, and only my wife seemed to grasp the extent of my distress.

During that time, I couldn't eat. Food tasted terrible. I would take a bite of something and chew it, but then I couldn't swallow it. I was losing weight fast. Fortunately, I had just signed on with a new health care professional after my previous doctor retired. My new APRN understood what I was going through because she had endured it herself. I came to her on a friend's recommendation, and what a thin thread that turned out to be. God often uses thin threads to bring about His desired outcomes.

My new APRN was able to do things my previous doctor couldn't—or wouldn't—do. My wife accompanied me on my first visit. I was utterly beside myself, not having slept for two days. While observing me, the APRN patiently read through the litany of symptoms that I was suffering from; that's right, I had made a list of my ailments, both real and imagined!

Following her assessment, she said, "I know what you're going through. I've been through it myself. Your nerves are completely fried." Over the next hour, she explained, in medical terms, what I was suffering from. It had much to do with serotonin levels and synapses that weren't firing. I had difficulty paying attention, but fortunately, my wife was there, and she was listening carefully.

My APRN assured me she could help me and that everything would be all right. She prescribed a new anxiety medication to be taken daily. I am not keen on medication, but I was desperate to get better. She explained that the new prescription would take seven to ten days to become fully effective. I wasn't sure I could survive that long!

The first night on the new medication, I was still unable to sleep. Every muscle in my body seemed to be firing at the same time. I was up pacing the floor, a plethora of random thoughts running through my head. I experienced esophageal spasms with symptoms resembling a heart attack. I even contemplated calling an ambulance. Eventually I got back into bed and closed my eyes, but I still couldn't sleep.

Praise God, my wife was there—kneeling at my bedside, holding my hand, and praying over me. That first night, she prayed over me without ceasing. I remember reciting the Lord's Prayer with her, along with other scriptural passages. My wife is well versed in Scripture, having spent most evenings reading her Bible while I was out and about "socializing" with friends. Her presence was a saving grace.

I managed only a couple of hours of sleep, and my anxiety levels were still through the roof. It took a full week before the new medication began to work—a long, grueling week for me and for my family. I felt especially sorry for my youngest daughter, who was still living at home while working and attending college. I felt as if I had become a heavy burden on my family.

Needless to say, I couldn't work during that time. Basically, I had become an invalid, lying on the couch all day for a month. Thankfully, I could still read, and with that, my wife began giving me books from her personal library. She had amassed a collection of spiritual and Christian books, which she began handing to me, one after another. Not only did she give me the books that she thought I needed to read, but she also gave them to me in the right order, each book built on the lessons of the last. Thus began a wonderful spiritual journey that continues to this day. I read twenty-five books that first month while lying on the couch.

One of the authors my wife introduced me to was Matthew Kelly, a Christian writer who started his writing and speaking career while still in his teens. Matthew Kelly began delving deeper into his faith when he was encouraged to do so by a family friend while attending Catholic Church in the suburbs of Sydney, Australia. At nineteen, he began speaking on Christian topics. Since then, he has written more than fifty books and traveled the world, sharing with audiences his love for Jesus.

The first of his books I read was *A Call to Joy*, which changed my life. I had always felt blessed by God, but I wasn't sure I had true joy. I longed for it more than anything else. In that book, I discovered that joy was possible even in the midst of illness. From that introduction, I went on to read several other titles by

Matthew Kelly, including *The Rhythm of Life, I Heard God Laugh,* and my favorite, *Rediscover Jesus.* In *Rediscover Jesus,* Matthew Kelly introduces a short prayer that spoke to me the first time I read it. I return to it often. It goes like this:

> Loving Father,
> Here I am.
> I trust that You have an incredible plan for me.
> Transform me. Transform my life.
> Everything is on the table.
> Take what you want to take and give what you want to give.
> Transform me into the person you created me to be,
> So I can live the life you envision for me.
> I hold nothing back;
> I am 100% available.
> How Can I help?
> Amen[1]

I first read this prayer in the depths of despair. The words rang true. I was desperate to make myself whole, to heal, and I knew that I needed God's help to do it. I began to realize that perhaps God had taken hold of me, shaking me to bring me back to the faith I had all but essentially abandoned. The good news was that, even through my self-exile from grace, I still loved Him deep down. I just wasn't sure He still loved me. Matthew Kelly reminded me that God loves me and forgives me, even though I had become a slave to the world. Try as I might, I could not escape Him.

As Matthew Kelly explains:

> Jesus is the inescapable friend who only ever wants your highest good. Everything that is good and desirable He wants for you even more than you want these good things for yourself.

---

1   Kelly, *Rediscover Jesus: An Invitation*, 103

It doesn't matter how rude you are to Him;
He will wait patiently, until you surrender to
the wisdom required to delve into the Jesus
question.[2]

Looking back, I believe God gave me just enough rope to hang myself—and I almost succeeded.

Benny Hinn, in his book *Good Morning, Holy Spirit,* wrote, "God is never early, but He is never late. Just about the time you think you're going to die, He shows up."[3] Even in the depths of despair, that sentence made me laugh. If you've ever been sick—and I mean really sick—you know how true those word are. God has a sense of humor.

Sometimes circumstances in life force us to look inward for answers the outside world cannot provide. As long as we remain comfortable, moving along a path of life filled with abundance, life becomes a noisy journey in which it's all too easy to ignore God.

Oswald Chambers writes:

> We never discover God until we come to a
> personal need for Him, and that drives us to
> Jesus. The whole meaning of life is that man
> discovers God for himself... We don't seem
> to need God until we come up against things.
> The basis for thinking with most of us is our
> ordinary logical common-sense, but when
> a man comes up against things he has to go
> deeper down than his common-sense, to fall
> back on something else, either fatalism or God.[4]

Although I felt as if I were dying, I wasn't being fatalistic. It wasn't predetermined that I should die yet. I still had some fight

---

2   Ibid., 28
3   Hinn, *Good Morning, Holy Spirit*
4   Chambers, *op. cit.,* 356

left in me, and with God's help, the support of my family, and the care of a very good APRN, I began a slow recovery.

The first thing I had to realize was that, despite my gross sins, I was still a worthy human being because God had redeemed me. Mother Teresa, in her book *Mother Teresa: No Greater Love*, wrote, "God's mercy is greater than our sins. He will forgive us."[5] She also prayed, "Lord, wash away my sins and cleanse me from all my iniquity."[6] I figured that if this prayer was good enough for Mother Teresa, it was good enough for me. Mother Teresa had put God first in her life, and I realized it was time for me to do the same. At that point, I was feeling worse physically and mentally than I ever had, but a quote by Mother Teresa helped me when I needed to hear it most: "The Lord has willed me to be here where I am. He will provide a solution."[7]

Recovery was slow. After about a week, the new medication began to work, and gradually we brought the anxiety under control. I praise God for the men and women whose vocation it was to develop that drug! If you've ever suffered an anxiety attack, you know you never want another one. Anxiety can have many triggers. For me, it was the four back-to-back heat waves we endured in August, which seriously disrupted my sleep. The failure of my previous medication surely added to the problem. Yet with my wife's patience and undying love, I slowly emerged from that time of deep darkness.

Only two people in my life ever led me out of darkness and toward the light of Jesus Christ. The first was Fr. Gene Barrette, of whom I have already spoken. God sent Fr. Gene to me at a time when I most needed Jesus, though I may not have realized it then. The only other person to have that same profound impact was my wife—and God sent her too. Somehow, He convinced her that I was worth saving!

Oswald Chambers writes:

---

5   Mother Teresa, *No Greater Love*, 112
6   Ibid., 117
7   Ibid., 31

> Whenever you come across a man or a woman
> who in your time of distress introduces you to
> Jesus Christ, you know you have struck the best
> friend you ever had, one who has opened up the
> way of life to you.[8]

I remember, early on in my illness, I was struggling with self-worth. Would God really save this gross sinner from the trials that I had brought upon myself? Lacking deep knowledge about God and my Christian faith, I was certain that I was unredeemable. I had lost all sense of self-worth and the meaning of Jesus's death on the Cross. Where had my belief gone? Where was my faith?

But then, I read this by Oswald Chambers:

> It is quite true to say "I can't live a holy life";
> but you can decide to let Jesus make you holy. "I
> can't do away with my past"; but you can decide
> to let Jesus do away with it... Jesus Christ can
> make my disposition as pure as His own. That
> is the claim of the Gospel.[9]

I had to let that sink in. That was when I began to remind myself that I am worthy because God had redeemed me through the death of His Son on the Cross.

I thought back to my catechism. I remember learning while I was young in the faith that, through the death of my Lord and Savior Jesus Christ, I had been sanctified and made holy. I remembered that even Saul (St. Paul) was forgiven for his sins as he persecuted and killed Jesus's followers! And what about King David? Hadn't he coveted his neighbor's wife and had her husband killed? An adulterer and a murderer, and yet God had forgiven him. Perhaps I had a shot at redemption as well. I began praying in earnest to the Holy Spirit.

---

8   Chambers, *op. cit.*, 1167
9   Chambers, *op. cit.*, 402

First, I prayed, "Come, Holy Spirit, help me to pray." Praying did not come easy to me. Even though I had been praying the Lord's Prayer and the Hail Mary all my life, I still felt awkward. Along the way, I learned the Prayer of Jabez and committed that to memory because it appealed to me on a personal level. Jabez realized he couldn't do it alone, so he begged God for assistance. But I wasn't ready yet to ask God for specific requests regarding my health.

Early in my illness, I was struggling simply to breathe. I wasn't able to breathe fully—another symptom of acute anxiety. As you might imagine, when a person feels like they're suffocating, it's hard to fall asleep. I became extremely claustrophobic in the darkness of my bedroom. I took to sleeping with a night light on, which helped. Then I began to pray the following: "Come, Holy Spirit, help me to breathe." SIowly, my requests became bolder as belief in my worthiness grew.

"Come Holy Spirit, help me to love like Jesus loves." Then, "Come, Holy Spirit, help me to forgive"—not only others but myself as well. My refusal to forgive had, in truth, made me a prisoner of my own design. This required a lot of work and soul-searching. An unwillingness to forgive is akin to drinking poison and expecting the other person to die. In reality, our unwillingness to forgive hurts us, not the other person. Eckhart Tolle writes:

> Forgiveness is to relinquish your grievance and so to let go of grief. It happens naturally once you realize that your grievance serves no purpose except to strengthen a false sense of self.[10]

Finally, I felt worthy enough to pray, "Come, Holy Spirit, help me to heal." I knew my healing would involve mind, body, and spirit, but my journey back to good health became, first and foremost, a spiritual journey. I first needed to fix what was wrong within me spiritually. I wanted to be healed in body, but I also wanted to be reunited with God. I began to accept that God still loved me and

---

10   Tolle, *The Power of Now: A Guide to Spiritual Enlightenment*, 120

would never will evil upon me. God is always good. God can't be bad, but He will let us be bad, if we so choose. I began to realize that, over the years, I had gradually let the devil back into my life. It's hard to defeat the enemy when the enemy has established outposts in your head.

FIVE

Learning To Live in the Now

For the first time in years, I had truly stopped. I had stopped being me. Now, with all this time on my hands, I began to dwell on my innumerable sins. I wondered if it was possible for me to live the rest of my life without sin. "Is it possible?" I asked myself. Then I wrote this note:

> Yes! it is possible if you make the devil let go;
> if you kick the devil out of your life. Let your
> being become One with the Holy Spirit, and
> the devil will be denied any point of entry into
> your life.

The thought seemed dubious at best, and I doubted whether I could ever put it into practice. Day after day, during my recovery, no matter how hard I tried, I failed miserably, slipping back into sinful and bitter thoughts. A sinner with a long history of sin cannot easily change behaviors that took years to develop. By then, however, I had read these words from Benny Hinn: "The Holy Spirit is present from the moment you ask the Lord Jesus Christ to forgive your sin and cleanse your heart."[1] Like Saul, I had to die to sin daily. I realized that there was no other path back to God. I like how Oswald Chambers puts it:

> Can God keep me from stumbling this second?
> Yes. Can he keep me from sin this second? Yes.

---

1   Hinn, *op. cit.*, 95

> Well, that is the whole of life, you cannot live
> for more than a second at a time. If God can
> keep you blameless for this second, He can do
> it the next. Let not your heart be troubled.[2]

I found reassurance and comfort in that passage. It's called living in the now, which is where God lives. Eckhart Tolle, in his book *The Power of Now*, has much to say on this subject. He says that what we perceive as precious—time—is not precious at all. It's that one point out of time that really matters—the now. This idea seemed to apply to my present situation:

> When you are ill or disabled, do not feel that you
> have failed in some way, do not feel guilty. Do
> not blame life for treating you unfairly, but do
> not blame yourself either... If you have a major
> illness, use it for enlightenment. Withdraw
> time from the illness. Do not give it any past
> or future. Let it force you into intense present
> moment awareness—and see what happens.[3]

Anyone who has ever been laid up with a major illness will tell you that it's not much fun. My thoughts were consumed with getting better, but before my body could heal, I needed to be made whole in spirit. This took prayer and deep introspection. With the help of God, I was beginning to find peace in my suffering—"the peace of God, which passes all understanding." Eckhart Tolle says the following:

> With this radiant peace comes the realization—
> not on the level of mind, but within the depth
> of your being—that you are indestructible,
> immortal. This is not a belief. It is absolute
> certainty that needs no external evidence or
> proof from some secondary source.[4]

---

2   Chambers, *op. cit.*, 683

3   Tolle, *op. cit.*, 218

4   Ibid., 22

We've all heard the saying "You need to live in the now." But have you ever tried to? It's not that easy. In fact, most people can't do it and don't know where to start. I was one of those people—too busy making a living and paying the bills to stop long enough to consider what "living in the now" even meant. My lifelong mantra has always been "Keep going—don't stop." I prided myself on being a model of efficiency, making every second of every day count. But here's what Eckhart Tolle has to say about that:

> Why is it [the Now] the most precious thing? Firstly, because it is the only thing. It's all there is. The eternal present is the space within which your whole life unfolds, the one factor that remains constant. Life is Now. There was never a time when your life was not Now, nor will there ever be. Secondly, the Now is the only point that can take you beyond the limited confines of the mind. It is your only point of access into the timeless and formless realm of Being.[5]

For me, that Being is God. God lives only in the now. God is light, and at the speed of light, time stands still. It is always now to God. That's why He knows everything and sees everything. Notice that the author capitalizes the word *Now*, like God. I believe God comes to us only in our "now."

If I want to be "one with the Holy Spirit," I need to be in the now. The great thing about being "one with the Holy Spirit" is that the Holy Spirit will never reject you. God the Father. God the Son. God the Holy Spirit. When we become "one with the Holy Spirit," the Holy Spirit leads us to the Son, and the Son shows us the Father. The Father and the Son dwell in heaven, but the Holy Spirit dwells within us. He moves throughout, touching every molecule in every cell of our body. In essence, we are Spirit. I seem to have missed that lesson in my catechism.

---

5   Ibid., 49

But why did I fall off a health cliff in the first place? Sure, I needed to restore my physical body, but I also needed to mend my spiritual body. What came first? Was it my physical ailment, or was it my spiritual ailment? Was it because I was living an immoral life while claiming to be a Christian? Or was it perhaps something much simpler, something that we really cannot see while we're in the midst of it.

Perhaps I was simply "content" with my life as it was. But was I lying to myself, or was I blind? Oswald Chambers explains:

> A man who is in moral harmony with himself,
> without being rightly related to Jesus is much
> nearer the devil than a bad living man.[6]

Looking back now, I knew that something was lacking—that there was a strange void in my life. I may have purposefully been inviting the devil into my life to fill that void, at every turn ignoring God and not filling that void with Him. I could have, and probably would have, continued on that course indefinitely had God not intervened. Perhaps it was time for God to do what He needed to do to bring me back into the light. Oswald Chambers puts it this way:

> There are prenatal forces of God at work in
> a man's life which he may be unconscious of
> for long enough; but at any moment there may
> break upon him the sudden consciousness
> of this incalculable, supernatural, surprising
> power that has got hold of his life before he has
> got hold of it himself.[7]

Something was stirring in my heart. I knew that I wanted something more—something better than what I had. I had been searching for that "something more" for quite some time, but what was it? Nothing I tried seemed to satisfy. I tried working out at the

---

6   Chambers, *op. cit.*, 1134
7   Ibid., 1290

gym, which lasted for about a year until COVID struck. I took up fly fishing, which I enjoyed, but I never seemed able to make time for it. I was always too busy working. Time and again, I told my wife, "I am praying for a God-given goal or objective." I kept turning to God for direction. Then I read this by Oswald Chambers:

> Do you want, more than you want your food, more than you want your sleep, more than you want anything under Heaven, or in Heaven, that Jesus Christ might so identify you with Himself that you are His first and last forever? God grant that the great longing desire of your heart may begin to awaken as it has never done, not only the desire for the forgiveness of sins, but for identification with Jesus Himself.[8]

Could that be it? Was God drawing me back to a holy life? If so, He was doing it in unexpected ways. But God's ways are usually unexpected—His ways are supernatural. My days of lingering in sports bars were over.

---

8   Ibid., 420

SIX

A New Lease on Life

Although I was still enduring sleepless nights, I felt like I had been given a new lease on life. By the grace of God, I was allowed to occupy this body for a little while longer. Only God knows when that lease will expire. When the time comes, I hope to be packed and ready to go! Meanwhile, there was much housecleaning to do.

You may recall that in the summer of 2025, New Englanders endured four consecutive heat waves. Their cumulative effect drove me over the edge. I had become frantic with anxiety. I could neither sleep nor eat. My wife was beside herself, trying to coax me into eating something, but often I couldn't even bear the sight of it! I was rapidly losing weight. While she worked tirelessly to nourish my body, she also nourished my mind and soul by placing in my hands many wholesome Christian books.

As I read, I began to believe that God had brought me to this point in my life for a specific reason. Like Matthew Kelly, I trusted there might be a plan behind it all—a plan involving miracles.

In *A Call to Joy*, Kelly writes:

> I struggled to remove the things from my life that I could now see were self-destructive and sinful. I saw that morality was not about right and wrong, but about life and death, joy and misery.[1]

---

1   Kelly, *A Call to Joy: Living in the Presence of God*, 8

It was also during this time that I read these words by Mother Teresa: "God loves me. I'm not here just to fill a place, just to be a number. He has chosen me for a purpose, I know it."[2] Could God indeed have a new plan for my life, a new purpose? Perhaps I needed to listen more closely to what He was trying to say. "We must recognize that God is good and that He calls us to what is best."[3]

Was I living what was truly "best" for my life? I knew I was not becoming a better person by sitting in a bar night after night, and I certainly wasn't growing in Spirit, though we occasionally talked about God and spirituality. In the words of Matthew Kelly, was I becoming the "best version of myself"?

Someone once told me that if you want to change some things in your life, you will need to change some things in your life! But what had held me back all those years? Why was I so unwilling to change? Was I too comfortable? Was I too lazy to set out on my own initiative? Was it fear, or was it a lack of respect for myself that kept me from moving forward? In his book *This Thing Called You*, Ernest Holmes writes, "Do not delay your good by thinking that you have so much evil to overcome."[4] Those words struck me right between the eyes!

Was I blocking God's good from flowing to me because I believed my sins were unforgiveable? I knew that He was fully aware of my gross sins, but I also knew from reading the Gospels that Jesus had died for me on the Cross. He who was without sin took upon Himself the sin of the world and nailed it to the Cross, so that each of us could be made whole and right with God.

It's called the Great Atonement, and it applies to us all. But then I couldn't help but realize that the problem lay not in God's willingness to forgive me but in my willingness to forgive myself. Many of us are racked with guilt, convinced we do not deserve His forgiveness. But that's nothing more than a lie that the devil wants us to believe. The Truth says otherwise, and the Word is the Truth.

---

2   Mother Teresa, *op. cit.*, 157

3   Chambers, *op. cit.*, 38

4   Holmes, *This Thing Called You*, 31

Jesus is the Word. What He says is the Truth. But what exactly does that mean for me? Clearly, my journey was leading me to a deeper understanding of God. The more I read the Gospels, the more comfortable I became with God the Father, God the Son, and God the Holy Spirit. The Bible began to make sense; I began to grasp the Truth as it is declared in the Gospel.

Oswald Chambers writes:

> Our attitude toward the Bible is a stupid one; we come to the Bible for proof of God's Existence, but the Bible has no meaning for us until we know God exists. The Bible states and affirms facts for the benefit of those who believe in God; those who don't believe in God can tear it to bits if they choose. People can dispute the words of the Bible if they like, But get a soul in whom the craving for God has come, and the words of the Bible create the new life in him.[5]

Have you ever met someone who asks you to prove that God really exists? I have. In the past, I simply walked away from such conversations because I know that a man convinced against his will is of the same opinion still.

Oswald Chambers explains it this way:

> An absurd thing to say is "Give me a text to prove it." You cannot give a text to prove one of God's revelations; you can only give a text to prove your simplification of those revelations. A text-proof is generally used to bolster up a personal spiritual affinity of my own.[6]

For the Bible to make sense, one must first believe in God. I did not have the privilege of attending a Christian college. I wish I had.

---

5   Chambers, *op. cit.*, 386
6   Ibid., 387

Instead, I went to an Ivy League school where most of my professors were atheists, and those who believe were afraid to talk about their faith. None of them ever bothered to talk to me about their faith or their beliefs (if they had any) probably because they were afraid of the law—you know, the so-called separation of church and state.

That law was never intended to protect the state from the church; rather, it was meant to protect the church from the state. Many of our forefathers came to America seeking freedom from state-imposed religion. That's not a matter of debate. It's the truth. Unfortunately, since the founding of this nation, laws designed to protect the church from the state have been twisted and misused to advance political agendas by those who would prefer we forget that this country was built upon Christian principles.

The irony is that today, most college professors consider themselves too intelligent to believe in God, much less in the Son of God. But high intelligence is often blinding.

Oswald Chambers argues:

> Let us get this fundamental distinction clear in our minds: we cannot penetrate the things of God and understand them by our intelligence; the only way we can understand the things of God is by the Spirit of God... We cannot think of a Being who had no beginning and no end; consequently men without the Spirit of God make a god out of ideas of their own.[7]

I've been a thinking man all my life; I consider myself a scientist and a reasonably intelligent human being. I enjoy learning about physics and earth sciences. I hold a master's degree in environmental studies and have been self-employed as an environmentalist for the past forty years. Yet despite all my education, I really didn't know who God was—or is. Why? Because I never ventured to know.

On my own, through thought alone, I could not rid my life of fear, regret, worry, and shame. During my illness, however, I came

---

7   Ibid., 200

to understand that these burdens resided not in my head but in my heart. So I began to pray: "Holy Spirit, help me to overcome my fear, my regrets, my worry, and my shame." God answered. He said, "Keep reading."

Someone once told me long ago: "The power of prayer; it eases the burden and it speeds the results." I remember thinking when I first heard those words, *Man, give me some of that!* Even an atheist would have to agree with such a statement. If the simple act of prayer can ease the burden and hasten the results, what harm could there be in trying? I thought Oswald Chambers put it clearly when he said:

> Prayer is an effort of the will, and Jesus Christ instructs us by using the word "ask." "Everyone that asketh receiveth." These words are an amazing revelation of the simplicity with which God would have us pray.[8]

Can prayer really be that simple? If so, why would I be foolish enough to shut the door in the face of God? In return for a little effort on my part, He promises to help me overcome. I am deeply moved by the words and actions of Mother Teresa. Even in her later years, she continued to pray, "Lord, increase my faith. Bless my efforts and my work now and forever."[9] Mother Teresa devoted herself to the poorest of the poor in Calcutta. Most of those she served were destitute and dying in the streets. Hers was a calling that only a few could answer, and yet she prayed for God to increase her faith—now and forever!

But why should I even want to increase my faith? Would it truly make a difference in my life? Ernest Holmes believed that a power flows through our words of faith. In fact, in his book *This Thing Called You*, he claimed there is a law of faith with the power to bring into your life everything you need. He wrote, "Faith can

---

8   Ibid., 709

9   Mother Teresa, *op. cit.*, 183

make you whole; Faith can convert fear into certainty, poverty into riches, disease into health."[10]

In the midst of my suffering, I committed that sentence to memory the moment I read it. My wife found *This Thing Called You* in a used book store and paid a dollar for it. She brought it home with the intention of reading it, but it sat unread in her personal library for months. It was one of the first books she gave me after I fell ill, and it spoke directly to me. I was beginning to trust in God once again.

In *A Call to Joy*, Matthew Kelly writes:

> Faith then is about trusting in God, seeking to
> know and understand His ways, and struggling
> to follow and live in His ways. This is the life of
> faith and the way to fulfillment.[11]

The Bible says, "As you have believed, so let it be done unto you" (Matthew 8:13 KJV). I admitted earlier that I had been bound merely by chains of unbelief, which I had placed upon myself with the help of the devil. Ernest Holmes wrote, "If you wish to be healed, you must expect to be made whole."[12]

I desperately wanted to be healed—that much I knew. For the first time in my life, I realized that to be full of health in body, I first needed to be full of health in Spirit. I had to be made whole BEFORE I could become well in body. I needed to pray.

Oswald Chambers says that the key, therefore, is prayer:

> To the natural man prayer is not practical.
> From the common sense point of view it is
> absurd. To the natural man who has not been
> born again, prayer is so simple and stupid as to
> be once "taboo."[13]

---

10 Holmes, *op. cit.*, 34

11 Kelly, *A Call to Joy: Living in the Presence of God*, 70

12 Holmes, *op. cit.*, 47

13 Chambers, *op. cit.*, 314

But prayer is not natural—it's supernatural. It relies entirely on God. Indeed, it is the working of the Holy Spirit within us. Chambers affirms this when he says:

> Prayer in the Spirit is not meditation, it is not
> reverie. It is being filled with the Holy Ghost
> Who brings us as we pray into perfect union
> with God.[14]

It is there that my spirit becomes one with the Holy Spirit. For most of us, this requires a tremendous effort of will. First, we need silence in which to pray. Our loud and busy world affords us little, if any, silence. That's how the devil wants it. The devil keeps us constantly on the move so we have no time to sit quietly with God.

Fortunately, I was forced into silence during my illness. I was home alone, lying on the couch day after day. No distractions, no noise, no television, no emails, no news feeds—nothing. I believe it was Mother Teresa who said, "In the silence of the heart God speaks."[15] We all need to find that silent place where we can close the door and talk with Him. Praying in silence is critical.

I probably never would have stopped long enough to venture into silence had I not fallen ill. In a strange way, I was actually glad I had become sick when I did. It forced me to stop and ask myself some hard questions—questions I didn't know the answers to after more than six decades of being me. "Call to me and I will answer you, and show you great and mighty things, things which you do not know" (Jeremiah 33:3). I was finally beginning to understand that I couldn't go it alone, nor did I want to. I was learning all over again that I needed to rely on Someone greater than myself. And it was at that moment that I came upon this paragraph in the *Complete Works of Oswald Chambers*:

> It is only when a man flounders beyond any
> grip of himself and cannot understand things

---

14 Ibid., 316
15 Mother Teresa, *op. cit.*, 54

that he really prays... As long as we are self-sufficient and complacent, we don't need to ask God for anything, we don't want Him; it is only when we know we are powerless that we are prepared to listen to Jesus Christ and to do what He says.[16]

My first question had been answered repeatedly in the books I read: Am I forgiven of my gross sins? The answer was yes. The next question was whether I could forgive those who trespassed against me. I am fairly good at forgiving people who have hurt me, yet I must admit there were still a few against whom I held a grudge—even feelings of vindictiveness. For my body to be restored and my Spirit to be made whole, I knew I would have to revisit those feelings with certain people.

---

16   . Ibid., 608

SEVEN

Moving on to Forgiveness

Matthew Kelly tells us in his book *Rediscover Jesus* that "there can be no peace without forgiveness."[1] Notice that he said NO PEACE. He didn't say that it would be difficult to achieve peace by failing to forgive. Rather, he said that *peace would not be possible without forgiveness*. He clarified this further by saying:

> Choosing not to forgive someone is like drinking poison and expecting the other person to die. When we choose not to forgive, we turn our backs on God and the best version of ourselves.[2]

By failing to forgive, we do more harm to ourselves than to the other person. To truly forgive someone who has wronged you is a decision of the heart. If you say "I forgive you" to another person, they may reject your message. But that's all right because in rejecting it, they're not hurting you—they are, in fact, hurting themselves. Forgiveness is a two-way street.

Have you ever said "I'm sorry" to someone, only to have the other person respond "It's okay, don't worry about it"? Holding a grudge is fruitless; it doesn't pay dividends. Clinging to your past hurts can negatively impact your mental, physical, and spiritual health by allowing stress and anxiety to build. Could my ongoing resentments toward certain people contributed to my tumble off

---

1   Kelly, *Rediscover Jesus: An Invitation*, 60
2   Ibid.

the health cliff? Could their unwillingness to forgive me have done the same? Perhaps? But over that I had some control. I could choose to forgive others, and just as importantly, I could choose to forgive myself.

I came to realize that by refusing to forgive myself, I was denying the very good that God had planned for me. He was trying to hand me beautiful gifts wrapped in ribbons and bows, and I was rejecting them in contempt for my undeserving self. How pitiful I must have looked in God's eyes.

Anyone who has ever been self-employed knows that the toughest boss he will ever face is himself. The same is true with forgiveness. I am more likely to forgive others than to forgive myself for the very same offense. What is that about? Why are we so hard on ourselves? Do I not trust myself?

In a *Call to Joy*, Matthew Kelly writes:

> Our lack of trust extends not only to other people and to material circumstances, but ultimately to God. We do not trust God. And because we do not trust God, we are unable to live in the present moment. Fear and worries fester in our minds, and weigh heavily on our hearts, preventing us from experiencing and enjoying the wonder of now.[3]

Eckhart Tolle echoes this sentiment in his book *The Power of Now*. In it he writes:

> The moment your attention turns to the Now, you feel a presence, a stillness, a peace. You no longer depend on the future for fulfillment and satisfaction—you don't look to it for salvation.[4]

---

3   Kelly, *A Call to Joy: Living in the Presence of God*, 119
4   Tolle, *op. cit.*, 68

If you want, you can replace the word *now* with "God." By living with God in the now, I no longer have to pursue my goals by myself. I am no longer beset by fear, anger, anxiety, stress, or discontent. I begin to incorporate God into all my plans and into all my decisions.

The many prayers that I wrote down when I was sick speak to the fact that I needed and wanted God back in my life, here and now. "Come, Holy Spirit, help me to make right decisions," I prayed. And "Come, Holy Spirit, take charge of my personal life." I had opened a direct channel to God through the Holy Spirit, and God was being merciful.

I began to ask, to seek, and to knock, and slowly God answered my prayers. I was improving physically and making great strides in my spiritual life. I found myself longing for fellowship with the Holy Spirit throughout the day, and He never once rejected me. The spiritual life is a beautiful thing, but God never forces His presence upon us. He cannot enter where He is not invited. I decided to swing the doors wide open and invite Him fully into my life.

As Oswald Chambers puts it, I had been awakened.

> Anything that awakens the strong emotions of a man will alter his mental outlook, e.g. the incoming of the Holy Spirit breaks every habit and every arranged set of ideas he has, and if he will only obey the Spirit, he can remake himself according to God's plan.[5]

Was there still time for me to become the person God intended me to be? By the time I had fallen ill, I believed I had already lived most of my life, and that conviction held me back—I though I was simply too late to be of use to Him. But then I recalled the parable of the laborer who arrived late to the harvest. The master sent him into the fields to work for the final hour of the day, and when all the laborers were paid, he received a full day's wage. Truly, he had

---

5   Chambers, *op. cit.,* 112

found favor with the master of the harvest. Perhaps I wasn't too late after all.

With that thought in mind, I began to develop a deep appreciation for my fellowship with the Holy Spirit. I called upon Him throughout the day for inspiration, guidance, and comfort. Slowly but surely, I grew more confident in my conversations with God. The Holy Spirit became to me like a loving, tender brother. I began to grow in peace, and my faith was strengthened. Perhaps I too could find favor with the Master.

EIGHT

Highly Blessed—Highly Favored

Ernest Holmes writes in *This Thing Called You*:

> Consciously commune with the Spirit and you
> will receive a direct answer... Communing with
> the Spirit you receive inspiration, you acquire
> confidence and faith, you rest in peace, you are
> poised.[1]

Aren't these the qualities we are all searching for? All these
qualities lead us toward happiness and wellness. When present,
these qualities replace feelings of depression, fear, anger, insecurity,
and unworthiness. What we are really talking about here is the
indwelling of the Holy Spirit.

Oswald Chambers puts it this way:

> God is Spirit. Therefore, if we are going to
> understand God, we must have the Spirit of
> God... My spirit has no power in itself to lay
> hold of God; but when the Spirit of God comes
> into my spirit, He energizes my spirit, then the
> rest depends on me.[2]

God will come in and energize your spirit if you invite Him in,
but after that, the rest is up to you. If you want to know true joy,
you have to get right with God. A lot of people believe they can

---

1   Holmes, *op. cit.,* 48
2   Chambers, *op. cit.,* 201

be satisfied without God. Many people succeed in living lives of happiness and pleasure, but only a few people experience real joy on a regular basis. Again, according to Oswald Chambers:

> Jesus Christ loved moral beauty, but he never said it would do. The natural virtues are a delight to God because He designed them, they are fine and noble, but behind them is a disposition which may cause a man's morality to go by the board. What Jesus Christ does in new birth is to put in a disposition that transforms morality into holiness. He came to put into man *who knows he needs it* [emphasis mine] His own heredity of holiness; to bring him into a Oneness with God which he never had through natural birth.[3]

It's a decision that every man and woman must eventually make on their own: "Will I trust in God or will I not?" It all boils down to a simple decision—and it's a decision that you can make now without waiting for God to grab you and shake you! But you have to know you need it—you have to want it.

In a *Call to Joy*, Matthew Kelly writes:

> It is most beneficial and necessary for us to surrender our plans and ambitions to God. This surrender frees us of our worries and anxieties, which are the result of our attachment to our ambitions and their material consequences. When we trust in God we become less attached to the material world, the Spirit begins to soar, and we grow in happiness—true happiness.[4]

---

3   Ibid., 348
4   Kelly, *A Call to Joy: Living in the Presence of God*, 120

True happiness is joy, and joy comes from the Holy Spirit. When I turn my back on God, I find despair, thereby rejecting joy in favor of misery, fear, regret, anger, worry, and shame. These are crippling emotions that always lead eventually to illness. Through fellowship with the Holy Spirit, I have the power to change all that.

Choosing fellowship with the Holy Spirit is a decision we all need to make. Oswald Chambers says this:

> The great thing that the Holy Spirit reveals is that the supernatural powers of God is ours through Jesus Christ, and if we receive the Holy Spirit He will teach us how to think as well as how to live.[5]

How many people have I met along the way who refuse to believe these simple truths? Unfortunately, when we associate with such people, we often begin to adopt their ideology and beliefs. Their suppositions become our suppositions. I have certainly witnessed this in my own life. My mother used to warn me, "Be careful who you hang around with, or you'll become like them." It's true; if you spend time with bank robbers, you will eventually rob a bank.

Indeed, the Spirit of God is everywhere—if only we would open our eyes. Seek and you shall find, or as Oswald Chambers puts it:

> The Spirit of God is everywhere, would that men would yield to Him. The reason we do not yield is that in the deep recesses of our hearts we prefer the captaincy of our own lives, we prefer to go our own way and refuse to let God govern... to disbelieve in anything but my own point of view.[6]

I have made some very poor decisions in my life by being self-reliant, by failing to include God in my plans. Some of those

---

5   Chambers, *op. cit.*, 123
6   Ibid., 124

mistakes led to substantial financial losses, along with the stress and anxiety that accompany them. As Oswald Chambers writes, "God rarely rebukes us for impulsive plans because those plans work their own distress. Plans made apart from trusting God's wisdom are rotten."[7] God doesn't punish us for being self-reliant—we do that to ourselves. But why choose that path when His will is for us to be joyful, happy, peaceful, and free from worry, despair, anxiety, and shame?

According to Oswald Chambers, we act wrong because we believe wrong.

> It has been a favorite belief in all ages that if only men were taught what good is, everyone would choose it; but history and human experience prove that that is not so. To know what good is is not to be good... To say that if I am persuaded a thing is wrong I won't do it is not true. The mutiny of human nature is that it will do it whether it is wrong or not. The problem in practical experience is not to know what is right, but to do it. My natural spirit may know a great many things, but I never can be what I know I ought to be until I receive the Life which has life in itself, the Holy Spirit.[8]

The Spirit of God is not some Being "out there." The Spirit of God lives within me now. The Spirit living within me is God. God the Father. God the Son. God the Holy Spirit. An infinite God capable of infinite forgiveness, infinite patience, infinite love, and infinite mercy. And what's truly amazing is that when we allow for the indwelling of the Holy Spirit, we gain access to the Infinite Mind that created the infinite universe, and that is astounding!

The Bible says, "Commit your works unto Jehovah, and thy purposes shall be established" (Proverbs 16:3 KJV). That simply

7   Ibid., 969
8   Ibid., 392

means to align your plans with God's will. In other words, include Him in all of your planning. In ALL of my planning? Yes—in ALL of your planning! Frankly, I'm sick and tired of going it alone. I'm sick and tired of making the mistakes that so often come from going it alone without God. According to Chambers:

> God seems to have a delightful way of upsetting things which we have calculated on without Him. We get into places and circumstances He never chose, and suddenly they are shaken and we find that we have been calculating on them without God.[9]

Indeed, early in my recovery from illness, I shook uncontrollably. On the night when my wife held my hand and prayed by my side, every muscle in my body seemed to fire at once. It was a horrible, intolerable experience that went on and on. In my anguish, I truly felt as though I might suffer a heart attack and die! In that moment, I longed urgently to let God back into my life.

Oswald Chambers sums it up this way:

> To take God into all our calculations is the one thing that keeps us from the possibility of worrying. According to the wisdom of this world, God seems to be haphazard. He is not calculable in His providence; He works in ways we cannot estimate. If we try to work things out in logical ways, we are apt to find that suddenly in the providence of God a great upheaval comes we had never calculated on.[10]

There is nothing wrong with having common sense. Living with common sense is better than living without it. Yet trying to face life's problems alone, apart from Jesus Christ, is a mistake. I've

---

9   Ibid., 443
10 Ibid.

tried going it alone, and I don't care for it at all. It's a very difficult road to travel. But when I take God into all my calculations, the road becomes easier.

Must everyone suffer to come to this realization? Perhaps not everyone, but it was certainly necessary for me—and for most of the people I know. Sometimes the only way God can get our attention is through suffering. Even Fr. Gene suffered excruciatingly.

In his book *Rediscover Jesus,* Matthew Kelly writes:

> I am not a fool enough to believe that my finite mind can comprehend the infinite Mind of God. Faith and hope lead me to the conclusion that suffering has value. I do not fully understand the reason or the value of suffering. Suffering is a mystery—and I am okay with that. Mystery is a beautiful thing. It shouldn't be scoffed at, but rather should be approached with reverence and awe.[11]

I believe that what Matthew Kelly is saying is true. But when you're in the midst of your deepest suffering, it is hard to approach life with reverence and awe. But like what Matthew Kelly points out, "The message of the world is incomplete, and nothing demonstrates this incompleteness more than the world's inability to make sense of suffering."[12]

Midway through my suffering, I found myself praying, "Come, Holy Spirit, help me to understand suffering." No one had to tell me that I was suffering. That much I knew. I was also certain that I wouldn't and couldn't get better on my own. Even my caring family wasn't enough, though I am very grateful for their loving assistance. I felt bad that they were being compelled to share in my suffering, and I was distressed by the burden I was placing upon them. I must have apologized a hundred times to my wife before she finally said, "Stop it!"

---

11 Kelly, *Rediscover Jesus: An Invitation,* 72
12 Ibid., 73

Little did I know that I was already on the road to joy. No one could have convinced me of it at the time, but like what Matthew Kelly explains in his book *A Call to Joy*:

> When I speak of joy, I am speaking of a state of mind and a condition of the heart that allows us to focus on a higher reality. The higher reality is the eternity of the soul and the soul's supreme reign over the body. And we can focus on this higher reality even when—perhaps especially when—we are sick.[13]

When I fell ill, I was reminded that I am nothing without God. I had learned that truth many years ago in my catechism, and it was something I taught my children as they grew and matured. I often reminded them that there would come a time in their lives when they would become absolutely dependent upon God—when no amount of self-awareness or inner strength would suffice. *It is an inevitability in every person's life.* The question is, will you be ready when it happens to you? As Matthew Kelly writes, "When we are involuntarily slowed down by illness, we are provided with plenty of time to pray, reflect, contemplate, make resolutions, and seek new directions in our lives."[14]

I was being forced, in a not-so-gentle way, to slow my life down. I was being compelled to reconsider my priorities, my goals, and my objectives. I was being pressed to refocus on the role God was meant to play in my life. I was being challenged to ask whether I still had enough time to become the person He intended me to be. As Kelly affirms, "Often an illness can be our passport to the higher state."[15]

On the nights when my wife knelt by my bed and prayed over me, she would say, "And thank you God for all the people who loved me and still do." At once, that became part of my daily prayer. How

---

13 Kelly, *A Call to Joy: Living in the Presence of God*, 129
14 Ibid.
15 Ibid., 130

could I have forgotten all those who loved me and helped me along the way? There were so many souls who contributed to my success in life and to the person I have become. I decided to compile a list of all those to whom I felt indebted for their love. There were many. The exercise proved cathartic and heartwarming. It made me feel better. Many of those who helped me have since passed on, but I can still feel their love in my heart. Love never dies.

Thank you, God, for all the people who love me and still do. I think of my parents and grandparents, my mother-in-law and father-in-law, Fr. Gene and Sister Mary Morris, my brother, and so many others who have gone to their eternal rest. They showed me their love while they were alive, and I believe they continue to show me their love now from a far better place. Matthew Kelly reminds us that "joy is the fruit of appreciation." He goes on to say, "If you want to know what to pray about or what to meditate on, this is it: the gifts in your life. Most of them are simple things that we take for granted everyday."[16]

Until we fall sick, we tend to take our good health for granted. When I was ill, I couldn't eat. Food tasted terrible. If I took a bite and put it in my mouth, I couldn't swallow it! That lasted for weeks, during which I lost more than twenty pounds! But then one day, everything changed. I was perhaps six weeks into my recovery when all of a sudden, food suddenly tasted wonderful. I felt as if I had been born again! Every meal became indescribably delicious— every bite a delight. Every time I reintroduced another food into my diet, it was as though I was tasting it for the first time. Food had never tasted so good!

> Come, Holy Spirit, help me to heal.
> Come, Holy Spirit, help me to eat.
> Come, Holy Spirit, nourish my body.
> Come, Holy Spirit, make me whole again.

Ernest Holmes wrote in *This Thing Called You*: "If you wish to be healed, you must expect to be made whole." Wellness and

---

16 Ibid., 124

wholeness go hand in hand. In fact, they depend upon one another. Recent medical studies reveal a close relationship between the mind and the gut biome, now called the Mind-Gut Axis. Researchers have identified a two-directional communication network linking the brain and the gut in ways not previously understood. As it turns out, our gut microbiome can influence digestion, immunity, mood swings, hormone production, and stress responses.

Two months into my illness, I realized I may have been suffering all along from a gut biome imbalance. Until that moment, I had no idea what the gut biome was, much less its role in the Mind-Gut Axis. Sometimes we must look deeper to understand the underlying causes of our illness. My APRN prescribed probiotic capsules, each containing one hundred billion CFU—culture-forming units. One hundred billion galaxies living in your gut to keep you healthy. Imagine that! I didn't know. Perhaps I had been asking the wrong questions all along!

You need to ask the right questions if you want the right answers. If you want to change some things in your life, then you must be willing to change some things in your life. Perhaps I had been asking the wrong questions all along regarding my wellness—or lack thereof. For that matter, perhaps I wasn't asking God the right questions either.

If I had known the right questions to ask my APRN, I might have recovered sooner. Likewise if I had asked God the right questions—if I had been more in touch with Him—I might have avoided falling off the health cliff in the first place. We refuse to realize that God is there for us all along, desiring to strengthen us in mind, body, and spirit. Oswald Chambers says:

> We ask with our eyes on the possibilities or on ourselves, [but] not on Jesus Christ. Get onto the supernatural line, remember that Jesus Christ is omniscient, and He says "If ye shall ask anything in my name, I will do it."[17]

---

17 Chambers, *op. cit.*, 237

Was I insulting God by focusing only on what I could do to get well, while ignoring Him? Perhaps. Was I willfully ignoring the doctor's orders? No. Did I ask questions of the medical professionals and heed their advice? Yes. Then why did I ignore God and the words of the wise? I now understand why. I was still holding myself back, clinging to the belief that I wasn't deserving of His love. Indeed, I had bound myself with chains of unbelief.

Through prayer, I discovered that those chains could be broken, and Satan could be sent flying back to the gates of Hell. Oswald Chambers reminded me:

> The prayer of the feeblest saint on earth who lives in the Spirit and keeps right with God is a terror to Satan. The very powers of darkness are paralyzed by prayer... No wonder Satan tries to keep our minds fussy in active work till we cannot think in prayer.[18]

"Come, Holy Spirit, help me to understand suffering." God was answering all my prayers. In the silence of my heart, He was speaking to me. From all of this suffering could come something good—something wonderful even. Jesus said, "I give you my joy so that your joy might be complete" (John 15:11 NIV). During my convalescence I read the Gospels six times through, and at last it was all beginning to make sense.

The joy I had not felt for the longest time—the joy I had withheld from myself because I believed I was undeserving—was suddenly being revealed. I could feel God filling my spirit with joy each time I communed with Him through the indwelling Holy Spirit. I began to long for this fellowship. As my faith grew, I sensed that I was being made whole, and with the return of wholeness came wellness. I had traveled through intense suffering to reach this point, and perhaps the very purpose of my suffering was that it was necessary for me to be made whole once again.

---

18 Ibid., 317

Matthew Kelly reminds us that Jesus Himself was made to suffer; why shouldn't I expect the same? A student is not greater than his teacher. Suffering is to be expected. Then why are we so surprised when it comes? Kelly writes:

> In the New Testament, Jesus boldly announced with His words and actions that suffering has value. It is a tool that can transform us into more loving people. It ushers us into higher spiritual realms. Salvation and the suffering of Jesus are inseparable. So what could be more meaningful that suffering?[19]

No one goes out of their way to bring suffering upon themselves. I hate feeling sick just like anyone else. I become a burden on my family, and that's not fair. Illness also interferes with the work that I have underway; it interferes with my productivity.

Yet being unwell forced me to stop. STOP. It compelled me to reconsider the choices I had made throughout my life—not all of them good and noble. Through my sickness, I was able to confront the true underlying causes of my fears, failures, anxieties, and regrets. Lying sick on the couch day after day, I grew increasingly interested in renewing my relationship with God. I was already reading every spiritual book I could find. I was devouring Scripture. And the more I read, the more I realized I really didn't know who Jesus is. Perhaps it was time for me to explore more deeply the meaning of Christ's death on the Cross. "For more than two thousand years," writes Kelly, "the heroes, champions and saints of Christianity have been meditating on the passion and death of Jesus Christ."[20]

"Come, Holy Spirit, help me to know more about Jesus."

---

19 Kelly, *Rediscover Jesus: An Invitation*, 74
20 Ibid.

NINE

Drowning in God's Love

For me, my illness brought in a blessed silence. The busy world around me came to a standstill. At first, it was unsettling and uncomfortable. I had lived with noise so long that I forgot what true silence sounded like. It was a welcome change once I became used to it. Matthew Kelly writes:

> If we cannot hear the voice of God in our lives, it is not because He is not speaking; it is because we are drowning His voice out with so much other useless noise. Silence is sacred and belongs not to this world but to the supernatural life. It is for this reason that people who spend time in silence are able to recognize supernatural realities while the eyes and ears of others remain closed.[1]

We are drowning out His voice. I am reminded that as a young boy, I nearly drowned in a boating accident, and the story has relevance because it speaks to silence, and to the voice we can sometimes discern during moments of extreme silence. When you're underwater, trapped beneath a capsized boat, everything grows still.

I had gone out on the river with a friend in his row boat. I was forbidden to go on the river at any time by my mother. I was not a strong swimmer at the time. But on that hot summer day, I ignored

---

1   Kelly, *A Call to Joy: Living in the Presence of God*, 138

my mother's admonitions and went out on the boat anyway. For whatever reason, at one point, I stood up and stepped on the side of the boat. It flipped, and suddenly I was in the water, beneath the overturned hull, in darkness and silence. I remember struggling repeatedly to reach the surface, only to strike my head against the boat each time. It was pitch black, there was no air, and the only sound was my muffled voice calling for help beneath the water.

As I struggled, I felt myself slipping into unconsciousness. I remember thinking, *This is it—I'm going to die today.* Suddenly, I was overcome with a sense of peace. I stopped struggling and lay face down in the water, like a dead man's float. It was perfectly silent, and I was no longer afraid of dying. Motionless, waiting for the end, I even opened my mouth to let the water in. I was ready to go to heaven.

Suddenly I heard a voice—someone speaking to me from within. It was my mother's voice, angry that I had gone out onto the river. I remember thinking at that moment, *If I die, my mother is going to be really hurt, and I do not want to be the cause of her pain.* So I decided to try again. I decided that I wanted to live.

While I lay perfectly still in the dark waters, believing I was dying, the river's current carried me out from beneath the capsized boat. Suddenly, there I was, on the surface in full sunshine, thrashing and gasping for air. My friend had already swum to shore and was yelling, "DuBois, climb onto the boat!" With that, I managed to drag myself from the water and onto the overturned boat. I would not die that day.

What struck me most was the calm that came when I accepted death. After several futile attempts to rise to the surface, I had resigned myself to death. In that silent darkness, I handed myself over to God. Only then was I freed from the entanglement of the overturned boat that had held me under. It wasn't until I stopped struggling and willfully turned myself over to God that the specter of death was lifted. I found myself in the light of day, released from the darkness, breathing fresh air once more.

I felt that God had saved me from an early death. I never told my mother what had happened to me on the river on that hot summer day. Was I grateful to God for saving my life that day? Of course I was. Did the experience turn me into a holy saint, never to sin again? Not a chance. In short order, I began relying on myself again. The real dangers we face come not from without but from within. As Oswald Chambers explains it:

> The majority of us are shockingly ignorant about ourselves simply because we will not allow the Spirit of God to reveal the enormous dangers that lie hidden in the center of our spirit. Jesus Christ taught that dangers never come from outside, but from within.[2]

When you're young, it's hard to discern the truth. It took me years of living life at full throttle before I realized that I was blocking the Holy Spirit from working out God's truth in my life. To discern the mind of God behind it all, I would need to endure more hardship.

______

2   Chambers, *op. cit.*, 179

TEN

The Mind of God

If you really want to understand the mind of God, don't go to college—unless you plan to focus on religious studies. There are some very good Christian colleges in this country, which I was not privileged to attend. I wish I had. Instead, I attended an Ivy League institution where my college professors were bereft of God's mind or anything spiritual for that matter.

In college, I studied science, where I was taught theories of relativism—where good and bad do not exist and can only be defined by the perspective of the observer. The theory of evolution was presented as fact, proven by science, and set forth as the antithesis of God's love. It should be pointed out that at the time, I accepted everything I was taught; I had taken the bait, hook, line, and sinker.

Oswald Chambers offers his own insight on this:

> Evolution is simply a working way of explaining the growth and development of anything. When evolution is made a fetish and taken to mean God, then call it "bosh"; but evolution in a species, in an idea, in teaching, is exactly what our Lord taught: born of the Spirit and going on 'till we all attain…unto the measure of the stature of the fullness of Christ.[1]

I borrowed a lot of money to finance my college education, convinced I was pursuing the profundities of truth and life. To me

---

1   Ibid., 540

the cost did not matter: if the dream was big enough, the facts didn't count. My college experiences proved rewarding and certainly educational, yet they also instilled in me a spirit of liberalism—a tolerance for everybody and everything. Upon graduation I stepped into life, handsomely educated but poorly enlightened.

It took many years of living in the real world to recognize that much of what I had swallowed in college was rotten, built entirely on false assumptions and bad data. Oswald Chambers writes:

> A bad man, an evil-minded man, is amazingly tolerant of everything and everyone no matter whether they are good or bad, Christian or not, but his power of action is paralyzed entirely. He is tolerant of everything—the devil, the flesh, the world, sin, and everything else. Jesus Christ never tolerated sin for a moment, and when His nature is getting its way in a soul the same intolerance is shown.[2]

It is difficult, if not impossible, to achieve a balanced college education today when most college professors are affirmed atheists. Where I went to college, believers were confined to the Divinity School, while any mention of God—or anything spiritual—was taboo.

During those years, I had one conversation with a classmate who didn't believe Jesus Christ was the Son of God. He did, however, admit that Jesus Christ was a great teacher. At the time, I was uninformed and immature in my faith, uncertain how to respond. It would take years of living and reading the works of brilliant Christian writers before I grew comfortable in my own spirituality. I remember when I first got my hand on a copy of C. S. Lewis's *The Case for Christianity*, in which he writes:

> I'm trying here to prevent anyone from saying
> the really silly thing that people often say about

---

2   Ibid., 154

Him: "I'm ready to accept Jesus as a great moral teacher, but I don't accept His claim to be God." That's the one thing we mustn't say. A man who was merely a man and said the sort of things Jesus said wouldn't be a great moral teacher. He'd either be a lunatic—on the level with the man who says he's a poached egg—or else he'd be the Devil of Hell. You must make your choice. Either this man was, and is, the Son of God; or else a madman or something worse. You can shut Him up for a fool, you can spit at Him and kill Him as a demon; or you can fall at His feet and call Him Lord and God. But don't let us come with any patronizing nonsense about His being a great human teacher. He hasn't left that open to us. He didn't intend to.[3]

In college, I was taught how to understand the world by thinking—by using my mind, my intellect, and my reasoning powers to explain what surrounded me. There is nothing wrong with that; it is logical, simple, and clear. Yet if I use my mind to explain what I see, shouldn't there be a mind behind it? Or are we too full of ourselves to recognize that truth? I like how Oswald Chambers puts it:

Atheism is what the Bible calls it; the belief of a fool. "The fool hath said in his heart, there is no God." (Psalm 53:1) An atheist is the one who says "I can explain by my mind *to a certain extent* [emphasis mine] what things are like outside, but there is not a mind behind that created them."[4]

---

3   Lewis, *The Case for Christianity*, 45
4   Chambers, *op. cit.*, 205

We all claim to understand the world around us "to a certain extent." Beyond that, such reasoning becomes contrary to logic and absurd. To a certain extent, we can grasp many things, but never fully. The real problem arises when a fool gets rid of God—he doesn't stop there. Oh no! He also does away with heaven and hell, right and wrong. First, we overlook evil. Then we permit it. Then we legalize it. Then we promote it. Then we celebrate it. Finally we persecute those who still call it evil. If you've been alive for the past twenty years, you've witnessed this process unfold across the world. It's the result of the great self-awareness movement—Godlessness.

Admittedly, I had seen this happening long before I fell ill. Yet it was during my convalescence, as I read and reread the New Testament, that I grew deeper in my understanding of who Jesus Christ really is. I realized I didn't have to tolerate evil because Jesus never tolerated evil. My college professors were wrong; I didn't have to accept sin in the world, no matter the form in which it appeared. Oswald Chambers helps by explaining it this way:

> In a spiritual soul this power of the soul will show itself in intense opposition to all sinful cravings. A soul that is born again does everything... for the glory of God... the whole mainspring of the soul's life is altered. This experience is true in every soul that is going on with God. When we are first introduced to the life of God there is a violent opposition to everything that used to be prevalent, and that it is so is not a mistake, it is what God intends, because there is the force of a totally new life.[5]

I have made my living in the forest products industry, among rough-and-tumble loggers clad in flannel and smelling of diesel. For the most part, they are hardworking, good-hearted, honest men and women, though their daily use of the English language is far from angelic. Having worked among them for four decades, I naturally

---

5   Ibid., 154

adopted the vernacular of the logger—the same oaths, used mostly for emphasis, like adjectives, but rarely in a demeaning way.

I do not slight these men and women in any way. In fact, I admire them for who they are and for the work they do. It's a difficult way to make a living. Yet during my convalescence I resolved to guard my words more carefully—I needed to clean up my act. Only when I stopped using vulgar language as part of my daily speech did I realize how much I had influenced those around me, including my daughters!

Whenever I heard either of my daughters use foul language, I felt hurt and offended. That was hypocritical, I know. But as I began to return to a new life of wholeness and wellness, I found myself increasingly offended by foul language wherever it came from. It seemed a small byproduct of my journey from suffering to salvation. Or, as Oswald Chambers put it, I was growing in "violent opposition" to everything that had once been prevalent in my life. Here's how he explains how my life had changed:

> How does this power show itself in a regenerated soul? It shows itself in opposition to worldly bondage... When you stand on this platform of God's grace, you see instantly that the bondage is in the world. The etiquette and standards of the world are an absolute bondage, and those who live in them are abject slaves, and yet the extraordinary thing is that when a worldly person sees anyone emancipated and under the yoke of the Lord Jesus Christ, he says that they are in bondage, whereas exactly the opposite is true. This power of the soul, then, when the soul is born again, manifests itself in opposition to worldly bondage.[6]

After eight weeks of illness, idled in silence, I resolved to abandon my worldly bondage once and for all. My diet shifted to

---

6   Ibid., 156

whole foods—fresh fruits and vegetables, less dairy, fewer processed items—and no alcohol. I began to work part-time again, but even walking around in the woods left me exhausted. Over time, as my condition improved, my appetite returned, and I began to gain weight, much to the relief of my worried wife.

Day by day, as my health improved, I sought a deeper understanding of the mind of God. To nurture that growth I became a voracious reader, devouring every title my wife placed before me.

Each day, as I grew in body and mind, I also grew in spirit—through reading and prayer. I began praying every morning at 7:00 a.m. with the help of a prayer app from Hallow, led by Jonathan Roumie, who plays Jesus in the powerful series *The Chosen*. My prayer sessions last only ten minutes, but they set the mood for the rest of my day. I've come to prioritize that morning prayer time. Oswald Chambers suggests setting aside time each morning to pray:

> Unless in the first waking moment of the day
> you learn to fling the door wide back and let
> God in, you will work on a wrong level all day;
> but swing the door wide open and pray to your
> Father in secret, and every public thing will be
> stamped with the presence of God.[7]

Every morning, I prayed, "Come, Holy Spirit, help me to surrender" and "Come, Holy Spirit, help me to praise the Father." In due time, I realized that all my prayers were being answered, one by one. I could feel God's joy pressing upon me. "I give you My joy so that your joy might be complete" (John 15:11).

I began to sense the power flowing through my words of faith. I confessed my growing faith to my family. Ernest Holmes writes in *This Thing Called You*: "There is a law of faith which has the power to bring into your life everything you need."[8] I realized I had been missing out on God's goodness because I was disobeying His laws.

---

7   Ibid., 1141
8   Holmes, *op. cit.*, 35

I needed and wanted a stronger prayer life if I hoped to understand the mind of God.

Prayer is evidence of striving to focus on God, of working to include Him in every decision, in every situation, and under every condition. Not surprisingly, the more I prayed, the more I grew in my faith, and the more I became aware of the Holy Spirit Almighty dwelling within me. The more I became aware of God's goodness inside me, the more I felt worthy of His forgiveness. I was finally leaving my feelings of unworthiness and despair behind me. Oswald Chambers writes:

> The measure of the salvation of Jesus is not that it does for the best man we know, but that it does for the worst and most sin-stained. There is no son of man that need despair, Jesus Christ can reproduce His saving work in any and every man, blessed be the Name of God.[9]

Being sick was no fun, but ultimately, I had brought it upon myself. I could not blame God or anyone else. God does not will evil. God is always good. But as I pointed out before, God won't stop you from inviting the devil into your life, if that's what you choose to do. "Come, Holy Spirit, strengthen me."

"Come, Holy Spirit, comfort me." "Come, Holy Spirit, protect me from evil." The Holy Spirit will never reject you. He longs for your fellowship. Pray in communion with the Holy Spirit every day. As Chambers says:

> Prayer is a complete emancipation, it keeps us on the spiritual plane. When you are at one with another mind there is a telepathic influence all the time, and when born from above the communion is between God and yourself.[10]

---

9   Chambers, *op. cit.*, 221
10 Ibid., 1050

It all comes down to prayer, for it is during our prayer time that we call to mind those things which God intends for us while releasing our yesterdays in favor of our tomorrows. "Forgetting those things which are behind, and reaching forward to those things which are ahead" (Philippians 3:13). It was time to give up my old, sinful ways and my infatuation with this temporal existence. It was time to focus on something much more important—the things of eternity.

Eternity. My illness had forced me to look deeply into the meaning of this word. I had already concluded that despite my gross sins, God considered me worthy of forgiveness. But what about eternity? Was I saved by God's grace forever? Yes. We have all been saved by the death of Christ on the Cross. Jesus's last words were "IT IS FINISHED." Once we accept this, we can all stand before God, free from sin and worthy of an eternal life with Him in heaven. Jesus said, "I solemnly assure you, the man who hears my word and has faith in Him who sent me, possesses eternal life" (John 5:24).

In all of the spiritual books that my wife had given me, the overarching theme was the same: I put God first in my life. I wanted that. I wanted to put God first in my life. I was searching for a better me—a better version of myself, as Matthew Kelly describes it. He says, "It is impossible to rediscover Jesus without rediscovering the Gospels. The gospels are a starting point, a primary source of rediscovery"[11]

While lying sick on the couch, I kept coming back to the Gospels. I found that reading the Gospels not only filled me with knowledge and insight, but it also brought me lasting peace and relaxation. The very act of reading the Gospels had a calming and soothing effect upon me. If you make the time to read the Gospels, you may find yourself becoming peacefully and happily centered.

Get your hands on a Bible if you don't already own one. Start by reading the New Testament. The New Testament is a great book filled with stories of love, encouragement, forgiveness, and God's Spirit. The message of Jesus Christ offends no one. If you're

---

11   Kelly, *Rediscover Jesus: An Invitation,* 118

offended by Jesus Christ, you haven't looked close enough. How can people find offense with Jesus Christ? Matthew Kelly answers:

> Somewhere along the way they were given a little bit of Christianity, and now they think they know all about it. Millions who have rejected Christianity have no idea what they have rejected.[12]

I call it becoming God conscious. When we become God conscious, we no longer have to rely on ourselves and on our own feeble strength as human beings. Instead, we can boldly call on God through the authority of the Holy Spirit. According to Benny Hinn, when you live your life conscious of God, you lack fear. Oswald Chambers says it the same way: "The remarkable thing about fearing God is that when you fear God you fear nothing else, whereas if you do not fear God you fear everything else."[13] Or, to put it another way: "Unbelief is a fretful, worrying, questioning, annoying self-centered spirit. To believe is to stop all this and let God work."[14]

Before falling ill, I was desperately ignorant that I imagined I understood myself thoroughly. I was delusional and in for a rude awakening. Remember what I said earlier: "God is never early, but He's never late. Just when you think you're going to die, He shows up." It's really quite pathetic how many people think they understand themselves with absolutely no knowledge of who Jesus Christ is and what He did for us on the Cross. As Chambers writes, "God is the only Being who can afford to be misunderstood; He deliberately stands aside and lets Himself be slandered and misrepresented."[15]

But why? Why doesn't He vindicate Himself? Because He wants us to choose. Freedom to choose—it's the ultimate expression of God's love. I believe that the worst condition a person can be in is

---

12 Ibid.
13 Chambers, *op. cit.*, 537
14 Ibid., 586
15 Ibid., 659

to never have the conviction of sin. A lot of people I know appear to have peaceful and happy lives while being totally dead to all the things that God represents. It is not until you experience the grace of Jesus Christ that you become convicted of sin by the Holy Spirit. And that is why Jesus Christ redeemed us by willingly going to the Cross. God is not going to redeem us—He has already redeemed us. All of us, you and me, all of mankind. It's the Good News of the Gospel.

And understand this: Jesus did not die because He felt sorry for you and me, nor was He a helpless victim of evil forces present during His time. Jesus died because He freely submitted to the will of the Father. He chose to obey God. As Oswald Chambers so eloquently puts it:

> The Cross is not the cross of a martyr: It is the mirror of the nature of God focused in one point of history. If I want to know what God is like, I see it in the Cross. Jesus Christ is not someone who leads me to God. He is God, or I have none.[16]

The Cross is the focal point of time and eternity. "He is not here, for He is risen" (Matthew 28:6).

The history of the universe pivoted on those few words. Two thousand years ago, the death and resurrection of Jesus Christ reset all measures of time and space. That simply doesn't make sense to an unbeliever, but never let common sense stand in the place of God's wisdom as it is explained in the Gospels. Nothing can ever separate us from God's love. As Oswald Chambers points out:

> Common sense is a gift which God gave to human nature; but it is not the Gift of His Son. Never enthrone common sense. The Son

---

16 Ibid., 110

detects the Father; common sense never yet detected the Father and never will.[17]

"Come, Holy Spirit, open my eyes that I may see." I am tired of walking alone in darkness. I want to have God by my side from now on. I invite God to be with me here and now, every moment of every day. But make no mistake, the path that God leads us on is a narrow path, and it's easy to fall off. I constantly pray through the Holy Spirit that God will take me by the hand and lead me along that narrow path and never let me go. "Without Me you can do nothing" (John 15:5).

I've been down the road without God too many times, and I cannot afford to do it any longer. I want to travel the rest of my life's journey with God by my side. I pray that you will find the time to rediscover Jesus and to invite Him back into your life.

As I sit by the fire writing these final thoughts, I am watching three logs burn. If you want to stay warm on a cold winter's night, it's best to stay close to the fire all the time. And if you intend to live a wholesome, loving, and caring life—the life that God intended for you to have—it's best to stay close to God the Father, God the Son, and God the Holy Spirit. It's not too late to become the person God intended you to be. I may be late to the harvest, but I'm here now—and that's where God lives.

---

17 Ibid., 1140

EPILOGUE

Remember, the Spirit of God dwells within each and every one of us. Let the Divine Presence guide, guard, protect, and comfort you. He will give you wisdom. He will support you in everything that you do that is in line with the will of the Father. "Ask, and it shall be given you; seek, and ye shall find; knock, and it shall be opened unto you" (Matthew 7:7).

By learning to talk with God, you will receive direct intuitive answers. Pay attention because God speaks mostly in soft tones. Remain in fellowship with the Holy Spirit. He is like a kind, gentle, and loving brother who leads you to Jesus Christ. He will never reject you.

Three months after tumbling off the health cliff, my journey to wholeness and wellness came to an end. I was back on my feet, going about my daily duties, back into the woods, and earning a living. I felt as if I had been delivered from a life of darkness, depression, fatigue, anger, addiction, and unworthiness. I felt like I had been born again.

It takes a lot of willpower to overcome these conditions, and it's not something that I could ever have done on my own. It also takes a lot of willpower to remain on the straight and narrow path—the path that leads to eternity. Every day, I struggle to stay on that path, but despite my best intentions, I sometimes fall off. But now I am acutely aware of my sins, and I strive to overcome them every day. It is the Holy Spirit dwelling within me that reminds me that the old me has been crucified with Christ, and now it is not I who live but Christ who lives in me.

Some days I live in holiness, in awe of all that God is. On other days, I find myself slipping back into my old self-centered ways. St. Paul said, "For the good that I would, I do not; but the evil which I would not, that I do" (Romans 7:19). Life has always been a struggle;

it's the very nature of life. But now I listen more closely to the Holy Spirit who dwells within, through whom God the Father and God the Son speak to me. I have gotten into the habit of being still during certain times in my day, listening for the soft voice of God.

According to Matthew Kelly, "The more you obey the inner voice, the clearer it becomes. But be assured from the outset that the Voice will make demands on you, will challenge you, and will ask you countless times a day to go against your lower animal instincts."[18]

I have come to accept my suffering for what it was, as it actually served a great purpose in my life. It sent me on a mind, body, and spiritual journey that I would likely have missed otherwise. It was a blessing in that respect. But according to Eckhart Tolle, it was more than that:

> The acceptance of suffering is a journey into death. Facing deep pain, allowing it to be, taking your attention into it, is to enter death consciously. When you have died this death, you realize there is no death—and there is nothing to fear.[19]

For me, the way back to the Cross was through suffering. At times, I felt as if I was being drawn back to God's kingdom, kicking and screaming! At last, I surrendered because I couldn't stand the pain any longer. In those precious moments spent in prayer with my wife, I chose to give up all control and self-reliance and to give myself wholly over to Jesus Christ. During my illness, I came to realize that what I truly wanted is what God wants for me. "Come, Holy Spirit, Thy will be done for my life."

After much suffering came blessed relief. I began to experience the kind of joy that only God can give us. God created us for it. In fact, God became incarnate in Jesus so that we could have complete

---

18 Kelly, *A Call to Joy: Living in the Presence of God*, 151
19 Tolle, *op. cit.*, 223

joy. "I have told you this so that My joy might be in you and your joy might be complete" (John 15:11).

If you want to feel this joy, make a point to read from the Gospels every day, for it was there that I found clarity, peace, comfort, and contentment. I watched my stress and anxiety slowly dissolve as a result.

If you read the Gospels a little every day, you will be led to the fulfillment of God's purpose for your life. You will no longer be bound by chains of unbelief. When your heart gets right with God, the Holy Gospel will become life and spirit to you.

Learn to be one with the Holy Spirit. If you are suffering through a crisis now, be thankful for it, and know that God loves you and He will never abandon you. Give yourself over to God.

BIBLIOGRAPHY

1. Hinn, Benny. *Good Morning Holy Spirit*. Nashville: Thomas Nelson Publishers, 2004.

2. Kelly, Matthew. *A Call to Joy: Living in the Presence of God*. New York: Beacon Publishing, 1999.

3. Homles, Ernest. *This Thing Called You*. New York: Penguin Group, 2004.

4. Lewis, C. S. *The Case for Christianity*. New York: Simon & Shuster, 1996.

5. Kelly, Mathew. *Rediscover Jesus: An Invitation*. New York: Beacon Publishing, 2015.

6. Tolle, Eckhart. *The Power of Now: A Guide to Spiritual Enlightenm*ent. Vancouver: Namaste Publishing, 2004.

7. Chambers, Oswald. *The Complete Works of Oswald Chambers*. Grand Rapids: Discover House, 2000.

8. Beneate, Becky and Durepos, Joseph, Editors. *Mother Teresa: No Greater Love*. New York: MJF Books, 1997.

ABOUT THE AUTHOR

Don DuBois has devoted most of his career to the environmental field. For more than forty years, he has served as a professional forest steward and land manager throughout southern New England. He continues to work as a private consulting forester while writing part-time. He lives In Connecticut with his wife.

www.ingramcontent.com/pod-product-compliance
Lightning Source LLC
Chambersburg PA
CBHW020643160726
47991CB00003B/992